Build a Flytrap

BY SAMANTHA S. BELL · ILLUSTRATED BY ROGER STEWART

The Child's World®
childsworld.com

Published by The Child's World®
1980 Lookout Drive · Mankato, MN 56003-1705
800-599-READ · www.childsworld.com

Acknowledgments
The Child's World®: Mary Swensen, Publishing Director
Red Line Editorial: Editorial direction and production
The Design Lab: Design

Photographs ©: Barnaby Chambers/Shutterstock Images, 4;
Mariia Tagirova/Shutterstock Images, 5; Melissa E. Dockstader/
Shutterstock Images, 6; Belozerova Daria/Shutterstock Images,
7; iStockphoto, 8; Shutterstock Images, 9

Design Elements: JosephTodaro/Texturevault; Shutterstock Images

ISBN 9781503807860

LCCN 2015958141

Printed in the United States of America
Mankato, MN
June, 2016
PA02301

ABOUT THE AUTHOR
Samantha S. Bell is the author of more than 30 nonfiction books for children. She loves spending time in her fly-free yard and garden in South Carolina.

ABOUT THE ILLUSTRATOR
Roger Stewart has been an artist and illustrator for more than 30 years. His first job involved drawing aircraft parts. Since then, he has worked in advertising, design, film, and publishing. Roger has lived in London, England, and Sydney, Australia, but he now lives on the southern coast of England.

Contents

CHAPTER ONE

Flies All Around

We see them at ball games, parades, and picnics. We see them on busy city streets and in farm buildings. We even see them in our homes! They are flies. No matter where you live, they are somewhere nearby. They buzz near our ears and crawl on our food.

Flies are drawn to many types of food.

There are many different kinds of flies. Houseflies are the most common ones found in homes. These flies are usually gray with dark stripes. Houseflies lay their eggs on old meat, rotten fruits and vegetables, and other garbage. When the eggs hatch, the **larvae** have plenty to eat.

Blowflies are another type of fly found in homes. They are sometimes called bottle flies because of their shiny blue or green color. Blowflies can also be shiny gray or black. When an animal dies, blowflies will

Some blowflies are shiny green.

find it. They fly around the animal and lay their eggs on it. After the eggs hatch, the larvae feed on the dead animal. If blowflies are in the home, it often means a mouse or bird died somewhere inside. Blowflies are also found near garbage cans.

Fruit flies are some of the smallest flies found in homes. Fruit flies are often light brown in color. Some have bright red eyes. Fruit flies are usually found in the kitchen. They are attracted to old fruits and vegetables. Soft drinks are also fruit fly favorites.

CHAPTER TWO

Dealing with Flies

Flies have quick life cycles. After flies mate, the female lays hundreds of eggs. The eggs hatch, and the tiny **maggots** start to feed. Once they are large enough, they find a dark place. There, the maggots turn into **pupae**. Inside a hard shell, they become adult flies. A fly can go from egg to larva to pupa to adult in just one to two weeks. They are then ready to mate and lay eggs. Up to 30,000 flies can come from one garbage can every week! With so many flies growing so fast, it seems as if they could fill up a house and a yard.

Flies can multiply quickly.

But flies are more than just pests. Flies can be a big problem. Some flies bite people and animals. Flies also carry **germs**. Flies land on garbage, rotting food, and other waste. Then they land on people's food or plates. They might land on a toothbrush or cup. Germs can go from the garbage to the fly to the person. One housefly can carry more than one million **bacteria**! The germs flies carry can make people sick.

Some people use sticky tape to trap flies. Flies land on the tape and get stuck.

There are ways to keep flies away. The first thing to do is clean up the places where flies lay eggs. Make sure there isn't any garbage or old food nearby. Many people use screens to help keep out flies. The flies can't get through the tiny holes. Other people use flyswatters to kill flies. Some people buy flytraps. Making your own flytrap is a good way to save money. Your homemade flytrap can work just as well as one from the store.

CHAPTER THREE

Flytraps and Nature

Sometimes there are a lot of flies in an area. There may be so many that people use chemicals to kill them. These chemicals are **poisonous**. They must be used correctly. If not, they can harm people and animals. The chemicals can also get on plants in nearby gardens. If people eat food from the plants, they may eat the chemicals, too.

Chemicals can also hurt helpful insects. Ladybugs, ground beetles, and soldier beetles eat other insects that harm our gardens. Honeybees make the honey

Some people use poisonous sprays to kill flies.

REDUCE AND REUSE

Water and soda often come in plastic bottles. Some people do not recycle the bottles. Instead, they throw away the empty bottles. Plastic bottles do not break down in nature. They will stay in the ground for at least 450 years! Making an empty bottle into a flytrap is a good way to reuse it.

we eat. They also **pollinate** flowers, vegetables, and fruit. These insects can be killed by the chemicals.

There are safer ways to get rid of flies. You can build a flytrap to catch the flies around your home. The flies go into the trap, but they can't get out again. Flytraps do not use chemicals. And they keep the flies from bugging you!

Honeybees are helpful insects that will not be hurt by your flytrap.

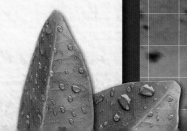

CHAPTER FOUR

Building a Flytrap

Different types of flies are trapped in different ways. This is because they are attracted to different things. Housefly and blowfly traps are similar. The bait is the only thing that changes. Fruit fly traps are different because fruit flies are smaller. All of these traps are made out of common materials. You might already have them at your home. You can buy any missing materials at a grocery store.

Once you've gathered your materials, find a place to work. You will be pouring and measuring liquids. So it's best to be in a place with a sink, such as your kitchen. Let's get started!

BLOWFLY TRAP

A blowfly trap is made the same way as a housefly trap. But you will want to change the bait. Blowflies are drawn to old meat. The meat will stink a lot. The stinkier it is, the better. Your trap will attract more blowflies with smelly meat.

MATERIALS

Housefly Trap

☐ Empty 2-Liter (.5 gallon) plastic soda bottle

☐ 1-cup (.24 L) liquid measuring cup

☐ 1-quart (.9 L) bowl

☐ .5 cup (.12 L) of maple syrup

☐ .5 cup (.12 L) of vinegar

☐ Spoon

Fruit Fly Trap

☐ 1-cup (.24 L) liquid measuring cup

☐ Mason jar or drinking glass

☐ .25-ounce (7 g) package of active dry yeast

☐ Teaspoon

☐ 1 teaspoon (5 mL) of sugar

☐ Plastic wrap

☐ Large rubber band

☐ Pencil

HOUSEFLY TRAP INSTRUCTIONS

STEP 1: Have an adult cut off the top third of the 2-liter (.5 gallon) bottle. Keep both parts. Rinse out the bottle with water.

STEP 2: Use the measuring cup to measure .5 cup (.12 L) of maple syrup. Pour it into the bowl.

STEP 3: Measure .5 cup (.12 L) of vinegar.

STEP 4: Add the vinegar to the syrup. Stir for about 15 seconds with a spoon until they are mixed together.

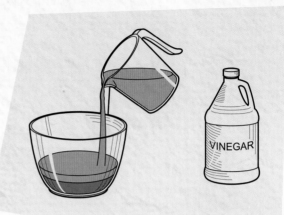

STEP 5: Add 1 cup (.24 L) of water to the mixture in the bowl. Stir with a spoon.

STEP 6: Pour the mixture into the bottom of the soda bottle.

PROTECTING HONEYBEES

Honeybees are important insects to have around. If you have honeybees near your home, you will want to keep them safe. Bees are attracted to sugar. Adding vinegar helps keep them out of your flytrap.

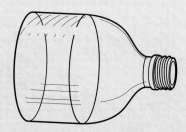

BE A SCIENTIST!

You can turn your flytrap into an experiment. First, decide which foods you think will attract the most flies. Houseflies are attracted to all kinds of food. You might try overripe apples or bananas. Some flies are attracted to potatoes. Keep a list of the types of food you use. Write down how many flies you catch with each one. Use your notes to decide which bait works best. Were you right about which foods would attract the most flies?

STEP 7: Turn the top of the soda bottle upside down. It should look like a **funnel**. Place it inside the bottom part of the soda bottle.

STEP 8: Flies will go through the opening to get to the mixture. Most of the time, they cannot find their way out again. Flies are attracted to light, so they will stay near the sides of the bottle. When the flies die, empty the bottle and start again.

FRUIT FLY TRAP INSTRUCTIONS

STEP 1: Measure .25 cups (.06 L) of warm water. Pour the water into the mason jar or glass.

STEP 2: Open the package of yeast. Pour the yeast into the water.

YEAST GETS ACTIVE!

Yeast is a type of fungus related to mushrooms. When added to warm water and sugar, the yeast becomes active. It breaks down the sugar for food. It releases gases. The gases make the yeast bubble up. Fruit flies are drawn to these gases.

STEP 3: Add one teaspoon of sugar to the yeast and water. The yeast will start to foam and grow.

STEP 4: Place a piece of plastic wrap tightly over the top of the jar or glass.

STEP 5: Put the rubber band around the jar or glass to hold the plastic wrap in place.

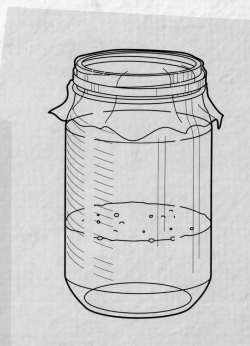

STEP 6: Using the tip of a pencil, poke several holes in the plastic wrap. The fruit flies will be attracted to the yeast. They will go through the holes to get to the yeast. Once inside, the flies won't be able to find their way out.

STEP 7: After about a week, take the flytrap outside. Empty it. Clean the trap with soap and water before starting again.

GLOSSARY

bacteria (back-TEER-ee-uh) Bacteria are a group of tiny living things that sometimes cause disease. Flies can carry bacteria that make people sick.

funnel (FUN-uhl) A funnel is an object shaped like a cone with a tube extending from the point. The top of the bottle acts like a funnel for flies.

germs (JERMS) Germs are microscopic living things that can cause diseases. Germs can cause the flu.

larvae (LAR-vee) Larvae are the worm-like form of many insects after they hatch from eggs. Fly larvae are called maggots.

maggots (MAG-uhts) Maggots are the larvae of flies. Maggots often eat old fruit.

poisonous (POI-zuh-nuhs) Something is poisonous if it contains a chemical that can harm a living thing. Many household cleaners and bug sprays are poisonous.

pollinate (POL-uh-neyt) To pollinate is to help plants reproduce. Bees and birds help pollinate flowers.

pupae (PYOO-pee) Pupae are insects in an inactive state of development, usually inside of a case or cocoon. Both flies and butterflies become pupae.

TO LEARN MORE

In the Library

Cronin, Doreen. *Diary of a Fly*. New York: HarperCollins, 2013.

Gleason, Carrie. *Everything Insects: All the Facts, Photos, and Fun to Make You Buzz*. Washington, DC: National Geographic Kids, 2015.

Murawski, Darlyne, and Nancy Honovich. *Ultimate Bugopedia: The Most Complete Bug Reference Ever*. Washington, DC: National Geographic Kids, 2013.

On the Web

Visit our Web site for links about flytraps:
childsworld.com/links

Note to Parents, Teachers, and Librarians:
We routinely verify our Web links to make sure
they are safe and active sites. So encourage
your readers to check them out!

INDEX